STILL A DEMOCRAT

Conservative Talk Radio Didn't Change That

STILL A DEMOCRAT

Conservative Talk Radio Didn't Change That

Scott T. Strain

Dedication

To my lovely wife Tara and our four beautiful children Preston, Connor, Jaxon and Lila Grace. Thanks for putting up with my craziness and wild ideas. You are all my world and inspire me to want more in life and to never be content.

Special thanks to Teresa Migliozzi Boyer who is an English teacher, freelance writer, editor and friend. Thank you for your time and dedication in being my official editor/proofreader. You are truly a special person. Thank you for your diligence and support.

Disclaimer:

The content in this book reflects my opinions and my opinions only. All quotes contained herein have come directly from listening to the conservative talk-radio show, <u>The Rush Limbaugh Show</u>© and have been properly credited as such throughout.

"I do not over-intellectualize the production process. I try to keep it simple: Tell the damned story."

—Tom Clancy, WD

Introduction

Welcome friends! My name is Scott Strain and I have written this book to offer my Democratic leaning insight on everyday conservatism. I attempted to subject myself to listening to far right-wing conservative radio for an entire month but didn't quite make it. Actually, the only show I listened to during this time was <u>The Rush Limbaugh Show</u>© and guess what? I'm still a proud Democrat. I chose this show for two reasons: he is the most controversial and I remember hearing from various people/sources who profess that listening to him would change my liberal leaning mind to the conservative way of thinking or should I say, the wrong way of thinking. I can tell you that nothing could be further from the truth. Listening to "The Big Mouth on the Right" only strengthened my resolve to remain a liberal and struck a spark in me to write this book so that my readers never subject their auditory senses to the likes of such useless drivel. And no, I'm not name-calling by calling him a big mouth rather I am just substituting a few words for what he really refers to himself as: "The Big Voice on the Right". In the pages ahead, you will see not only how he sees himself but how he views those who do not align themselves with the conservative way of thinking. And by "those" I mean all liberals in general.

I actually embarked upon writing this book several years ago then switched to writing my own blog and finally, just stopped doing any of it. I didn't stop for any particular reason; I guess I just became uninspired. As time went on, I always had it in the back of my mind to write this book and finally, I put pen to paper. Simply stated, I couldn't stomach his right wing, over-the-top, conservative rhetoric. I'm sure that once in publication, Rush and his team may try to discredit what I've written about which I fully expect, however, I am only offering my opinions as it pertains to direct quotes I have either heard him state live on-air or what I've read from his show transcripts on the days I may have only heard a snippet or two from his show. Now, in full disclosure, I do listen to his radio show from time to time and started doing so a few years ago, but only to remind myself as to why I remain a left leaning, level headed American.

As a matter of fact, it was in February 2012 that I had first listened to his program. I remember that day vividly as this was what went on to be one of his many infamous rants of ignorance at its best moments involving law student Sandra Fluke. I remember thinking to myself "This just can't be a real show about real political issues." It just seemed it couldn't be a bonafide radio program, but of course, I knew otherwise. If you don't recall the ignorant lump going after Sandra Fluke and the media frenzy that ensued after his comments, allow me to refresh your memory on the pages that follow.

But first, let me thank you for indulging me for a short, but serious look into the political spectrum, that which is called conservative radio. For this, I am greatly humbled yet excited to share my thoughts with all of you.

WHY I'M A DEMOCRAT

Before I delve into my experiences listening to the conservative circus of a talk radio show, I thought I would share why it is that I am a Democrat. It is truly a decision I made on my own. Although raised in a blue collar town with a blue collar working father and stay at home mother of whom were Democrats, they were not all that enthralled with politics. They rarely discussed political issues and when it came time to vote, they voted the democratic ticket every time. That pretty much sums up the influence my parents had on me as it pertains to politics. That and my Mom always saying that President Bill Clinton was her favorite President.

So I went through my young adult life and into my adult life not really caring what was going on in the world of politics. After getting married to my beautiful wife Tara, I came to the realization that the government and the decisions our elected officials made on a daily basis really did affect my life. Hence, I began to pay more attention to what the issues were, who stood for what, so on and so forth. And wouldn't you know it, the year I decide to finally follow the political goings on is the same year that the Bush/Gore election took place and the debacle in Florida occurred with counting votes. This soured me and my taste for politics, but I kept myself informed anyway and slowly became a political junkie of sorts.

To answer the question as to why I'm a Democrat though is simple. I strongly believe that there is a need for the regulatory arm of the United States Government. Agencies such as the Internal Revenue Service, the Department of Education, the Environmental Protection Agency, etc. are all necessary in order to help maintain this great nation as being just that, great. I also believe in the social programs such as welfare, social security, health care, etc. as to protect and care for our citizens at a time when it is most needed in their lives. Do I think that every program and regulating arm of the government is perfect? Absolutely not, however I do believe they are still necessary. I do believe that reforms that make sense are needed but not to the extent to where these agencies and programs are simply done away with and the people they support discarded like yesterday's trash. We all know and would agree that waste and abuse occurs within these programs which is where I think common sense reforms could help to combat this. I'm also quite certain that we could agree that waste and abuse occurs within the confines of the Wall Street establishment, but I don't hear Republicans calling for them to be shut down. To do so would be ludicrous and detrimental to everyday life in the United States of America. This same thought applies to government agencies and social programs as well. Republicans however think otherwise.

Conservatives don't have the same belief system. I've heard conservatives, some famous and some just around my small town of Girard, Ohio say that the Department of Education should be disbanded altogether and have further stated that the same should happen to the IRS and EPA to name a few. Really? Get rid of these agencies simply because conservatives think they are too intrusive to the citizens of this great country? If they offered at least reasonable solutions and/or replacements, then maybe consideration could be given but to simply say "Get rid of them" is not the answer anyone with half a brain would even consider. I, for one, am personally thankful for the Department of Education, as without the Federal loans and grants available; I would not have been able to complete my college education, which by the way I believe every American should be given this opportunity, regardless of their financial status. The Department of Education makes that possible.

This is only a few examples of their radical ideas in order to have "less government intrusion" as they say. Well folks, I could not disagree more and could never find myself entangled in the conservative ideology. I could just not allow myself to ever have this belief system.

MY FIRST RUSH EXPERIENCE

SANDRA FLUKE 2-29-2012

RUSH LIMBAUGH: *"What does it say about the college co-ed Susan Fluke [sic] who goes before a congressional committee and essentially says that she must be paid to have sex -- what does that make her? It makes her a slut, right? It makes her a prostitute. She wants to be paid to have sex. She's having so much sex she can't afford the contraception. She wants you and me and the taxpayers to pay her to have sex."* [Source: The Rush Limbaugh Show 2-29-2012]

RUSH LIMBAUGH: *"So Miss Fluke and the rest of you feminazis, here's the deal: If we are going to pay for your contraceptives and thus pay for you to have sex, we want something. We want you to post the videos online so we can all watch."* [The Rush Limbaugh Show 2-29-2012]

And so it began. The quotes above were my first full experience of listening to The Rush Limbaugh Show, well before diving in with both feet and making the decision to challenge myself to write this book. If the saying "First impressions are lasting impressions" were ever more true, I cannot recall. As you can imagine, I was not only appalled, but shocked. I was shocked that he would say such things. I was shocked that he has such a wide listening base as, from what I've heard or read, it is over millions of listeners a day. I was shocked to know that this is what this man has made many millions of dollars for doing. I then took a breath as I felt my blood pressure rise and was shocked again. Shocked at myself for even being shocked. I, of course, had seen reports over the years about Rush and his radio antics. I had read the stories from the past, or should I say skimmed the stories, about the shock value of what he says. Once I realized this and put things into perspective, I resolved to myself that he is simply behind that microphone to entertain the masses not to offer anything of substance.

Now, back to the ignorance that which are the quoted lines that began my first Rush experience. The reason behind his rant was because Sandra Fluke thought it wrong that her college health plan didn't cover contraception and of course, Mr. Limbaugh turns this into a "low educated" liberal argument. What he says about liberals and liberalism is a total farce, however, he pontificates about how he knows liberals and their beliefs better then we know them ourselves. And wouldn't you know the listening audience, at least those few callers who actually make it on his show, take the bait and stroke his ego as if he were a God. This, by the way, is how he portrays himself. He, in his mind and his followers' minds, see him as beautiful political mind. I'm sorry, but it just isn't so. I am in no way implying that Rush is dumb or lacks gray matter, however, I am saying that he is not solving any of the political problems he drones on and on about. He is simply creating a further divide among those who are liberals and those who are conservatives. Does he really want the masses to believe that he thinks that Ms. Fluke is a slut or that he wants videos of the sexual escapades in return for contraception to be covered? No, but he does want the word to get out that he made these outlandish comments and the media to talk about him. This is what drives his business. The more shocking he is, the more attention he garners which leads to growing the curiosity of the general public by which directs them to want to check out his show. That's all it is folks. It's not substantive ideas he is speaking of, rather it is shock value to generate business and listeners, which puts serious coin in his already deep pockets. The idea is simple and that idea is marketing. If he can maintain the millions of listeners coming back to listen to his three hours of bogus nonsense every day, the more he will make from his sponsors. Those who advertise with him only care about the bottom line. Unfortunately, that bottom line is an advertiser being able to reach an audience that is vast and provides full potential for their product to get sold. What better way than advertise on a show that reaches the masses. Hell, one may say if shock equals business generation which equals making the shock host a multimillionaire, Limbaugh is a genius. Lord knows he thinks he is.

BEFORE MY LISTENING JOURNEY

The Fluke story and the new level of ignorance I now knew existed because of Mr. Limbaugh inspired me to want to speak out against this man but I just wasn't sure how. I thought maybe a blog or a simple social media page dedicated to shedding light on what Limbaugh spewed five days a week, three hours a day could make a difference. So I decided on a writing a blog utilizing a free site. I followed through with this avenue for a few weeks, but in the end, I knew it wasn't the path I wanted to take. I just couldn't figure out why he was so popular, but then again, he is the political equivalent of shock jock Howard Stern, no offense Mr. Stern. Rush spouts off at the mouth in order to garner the attention of the main stream news media of which he claims to despise yet says these things to attract their attention. It's all a game and one at which has made this man very popular among the conservatives. Now don't misunderstand, I am all for capitalism and being successful at whatever craft you choose. I just have a hard time comprehending how he carries such a large audience and because of this, carries the sponsors of whom are the reason for his millions. I have many conservative friends to include those who align themselves with the Tea Party who tell me that they can't even stand to listen to Limbaugh.

For the reasons outlined above, my own personal convictions and out of shear morbid curiosity, I decided to undertake listening to his show for thirty days and by the end of this book, you will see why I only lasted a fraction of my intended goal. I considered coming up with various names, derogatory and otherwise, to describe Limbaugh, but figured why stoop to his level. You'll see what I mean by "his level" in the chapters that follow with the final chapter giving you perceived definitions of the labels/name calling tactics he places on those who don't align themselves with his conservative beliefs.

And so the journey begins.....

"If a free society cannot help the many who are poor, it cannot save the few who are rich."

~John F. Kennedy

DAY 1

JANUARY 26th, 2015

My first day listening. Going into this excited because I have psyched myself up for this experience knowing that the end result would be a lighthearted look at conservatism through the blue collar eyes of a guy like me having listened to the ever popular alleged voice of the right, Rush Limbaugh. I also went into this first day after having mulled over in my mind the difference between being a liberal and being a conservative and coming to the conclusion that being a liberal democrat just makes sense to me and aligns with my ideals and moral fabric. Now, I'd be a liar if I told you I've never been ridiculed or been told that I'm uniformed simply because of my political affiliation, however, I'm not ever phased by it, nor has it ever changed my political convictions.

After having said all that, I find this first show to be the perfect show to have started my journey. It's Limbaugh going on about Governor Scott Walker of Wisconsin and how he is just right for the Republican Party. Rush, in his self-proclaimed infinite wisdom says;

RUSH LIMBAUGH: *"And you know me, folks, if you have spent any time listening to this program in the last two years, you know that I believe Scott Walker is the blueprint for the Republican Party if they are serious about beating the left."* [The Rush Limbaugh Show 1-26-2015]

I found this fascinating as I was very aware of Scott Walker's feeling towards labor unions where saying he dislikes them would be an understatement. Walker, unfortunately, was successful in going after collective bargaining wherein it tied the hands of those involved and those employed under collective bargaining agreements and prevented them from bargaining freely. Those involved would have to abide by very stringent bargaining guidelines to the point where it wouldn't really makes sense to negotiate. It was a way, in my view as well as many others, to break unions altogether. What was even more disheartening was that the State Supreme Court upheld this nonsense.

Why is this important? Well, as you know, labor unions are plentiful and let's face it, the larger unions, such as the ones that protect those who work for large manufacturers of automobiles for example, have political power that comes in the form of money and endorsements. Does Walker really believe that upsetting the apple cart as it pertains to union organizations is going to be good for anyone's campaign? My answer is always going to be in the negative, but not in his eyes, or any conservatives' eyes for that matter. To them organized labor takes away individuality and prevents business managers and CEO's the power to run their company. The reality of it all is that unions negotiate fair wages, safe workplaces, and fair medical insurance. I know this because I have worked both in a union and as a manager where I had to work with union officials. The two key words are "negotiate" and "fair." Negotiating details to a mutual agreement and understanding while keeping the terms of the contractual language fair is what it's all about. To say that I believe that Walker doesn't have a prayer at any nomination given his seemingly vexed feelings towards labor unions would not only be accurate, but would be a certain truth.

Quick note: As of the writing of this book, Gov. Scott Walker has since suspended his campaign for the Republican nominee for President. In other words, he dropped out and Rush's epiphany that Walker had the blueprint for the Republican Party to beat the left was not only wrong, but was in fact preposterous.

We could hope that the other Republican candidates thought Rush to be right about Walker having the Republican blueprint to beat liberals. Those candidates who follow said blueprint would most likely meet the same fate as Walker thereby virtually giving any political office to a Democrat without the political back and forth nonsense.

"Human kindness has never weakened the stamina or softened the fiber of a free people. A nation does not have to be cruel to be tough."

~*Franklin D. Roosevelt*

DAY 2

FEBRUARY 2nd, 2015

Something as arbitrary as what fast food restaurants serve and don't serve is not safe from the jowls of this man. This particular day he was referring to a fast food chain and the movement out there to get them to change or at least add healthier food options to their menus. Rather than discuss this topic like a normal human being on an intelligent level, he resorts to name-calling and childish rants. And of course, it's all because of liberalism and the "crazy" left. This is what he had to say:

RUSH LIMBAUGH: *"Militant vegans, militant vegetarians, are attempting not to get McDonald's to serve food they want to eat because they're never gonna go to McDonald's. They're trying to shut McDonald's down just like they tried to shut Burger King down in Berkeley by making 'em sell veggie burgers out there in the fast-food lane or whatever. You start appeasing the left... I don't care if you're the Republican Party or if you're McDonald's. If you start appeasing them, you try to make them happy... One of the things they do... They've perfected this. McDonald's ended up thinking that half the country was ticked off at 'em for serving unhealthy food, and it was probably 12 people. Twelve people making themselves look like they were 300,000 people with* *weird Twitter algorithms and whatever other kinds of abuses they engage in, and we know this because they do it to us."* [The Rush Limbaugh Show 2-2-2015]

This is how Rush Limbaugh has an intelligent conversation with his audience. It can't just be a debate about the true reason for concern, which is to at least offer healthy food options, he has to turn it into some drastic liberal argument that really doesn't exist but in his mind. Look at the terminology he uses or should I say elementary name-calling contest he has with himself. He can't just refer to those raising the issues as vegans or vegetarians, he as to insert the term militant as if this describes the Democrat party, whether in part or as a whole. Look closely at the end of the quote where he says we, as a party, "engage in abuses and it's what's they (liberals) do to them (conservatives)." I believe this not only begs, but cries the question "Is not the language you use towards liberals and the Democratic party in and of itself being verbally abusive?" The answer is most certainly "yes!"

He goes on further in his tirade or dialogue, whatever you want to call it to say:

RUSH LIMBAUGH: *"They're not trying to help McDonald's. They're not trying to make McDonald's a healthier restaurant. They're trying to shut McDonald's down. That is their objective. On the militant left -- I don't care if it's vegans, if it's vegetarians, if it's environmentalist* *wackos, if it's feminazis -- there is no desire to work together to compromise to take their enemies or their opponents and straighten 'em out and make 'em right. They want to shut everybody down. It's like Obama"* [The Rush Limbaugh Show 2-2-2015]

As you can see, his words only become more harsh towards the Democrats and paints all of us affiliated with liberalism with one broad brush. And it wouldn't be Rush if he didn't somehow point all of this to our beloved President of the United States, Barack Obama. Look at his flat out lack of wanting to even try to see this issue from a different perspective. Obesity is a real problem in the United States. Hell, I am one of those statistics of being obese. Not proud of it, I just like food but I digress. He correlates this movement with liberals trying to close down a franchise, not help them. He portrays the idea to add healthy food options to the menu as liberals desire to shut them down. He ends with comparing this to how President Obama operates, which is no surprise since he was the one who said he hopes President Obama fails when he won his first Presidential election. That was all over the news then and he stills spews this hatred for him now, just in many different forms. But his angry-all-the-time and constipated-esque demeanor has to get old, even for him. Maybe if he had healthier food options that included foods higher in fiber from fast food restaurant establishments, it would rid him of his obstinate, ill feelings towards us and help him to shed the constipation type attitude altogether. In other words, maybe he could use a good cleanse to include flushing himself of his hateful, vengeful attitude towards Democrats. But just in the short time I've listened to his program, I'm sure Rush's response would be something along the lines of him being too good to even dine at such places.

"Tolerance implies no lack of commitment to one's own beliefs. Rather it condemns the oppression or persecution of others."

~John F. Kennedy

DAY 3

FEBRUARY 3rd, 2015

Football. This is my beloved sport to watch, especially college football. Sadly, the beloved game of football can't even hide from the grips of Limbaugh. Yes folks, Rush set his sights on football and the so-called controversial call in the Superbowl where the Seattle Seahawks decided to pass the ball instead of letting Marshawn Lynch attempt to run the ball into the end zone for the score to win Superbowl XLIX. The end result, as if you didn't know, was an interception and the Patriots become the Superbowl champs. Well, wouldn't you know that the story-line found its way into the Big Mouth on the Right's hands or should I say his jowls and he illustrates that the reason it's even a story is the fault of liberals. The headlines were everywhere and all were begging the question as to why the coach made the decision he did and why didn't the coach just give the ball to his star running back and so on and so forth. Well, the not-so-friendly conservative had this to say when he seems to be telling his audience why the play call was considered racist by liberals:

RUSH: *"Well, why does it make no sense? Well, I'll explain it if you just sit there and be patient. I'll explain it from the left's perverted thought process, I'll tell you how that call was racist. The call was racist not to give the ball to Marshawn Lynch and instead give it to Russell Wilson because the Seahawks and Coach Carroll think that Wilson is a much cleaner cut black guy. He's a more wholesome black guy than Marshawn Lynch. He's not as dark as Marshawn Lynch, liberals do, and they have now said that they got a source in the Seahawks locker room that told them this, an unnamed source."* [The Rush Limbaugh Show 2-3-2015]

Well, there you have it. Limbaugh summed it up in just a few short sentences so I guess it must be true and accurate. Problem solved and questions answered, right? Absolutely not. This guy can find a problem in anything and make sure his audience firmly believes that whatever goes wrong in this world, it's the Democrats fault. You could find a cute little child eating blue cotton candy and he would have you believe that the liberals must have the corner on the cotton candy market because the cotton candy was blue, the traditional color that represents Democrats. It must be the liberals' trying to indoctrinate children at an early age by selling them Democratic blue cotton candy is what his story-line would be. Far-fetched maybe, but he can seriously turn any headline out there and find a minuscule reason as to why the thinking is wrong and how it's a liberals fault to begin with. This is what he does on a daily basis. He doesn't shed light on why it's so great to be a conservative, nor does he, in my opinion, make it appealing to want to be conservative. I'm only on Day 3 of this talk-radio journey and it seems that if what he represents is conservatism, then I'm not buying it. It is apparent to me that being miserable is what it means to be a conservative. I'm not implying all conservatives by any stretch of the imagination are miserable, however, Rush is the self-proclaimed face of the conservative brand and misery seems to be the spirit of his brand. Sorry sir, I prefer to be happy.

"I believe that, as long as there is plenty, poverty is evil."

~Robert Kennedy

DAY 4

FEBRUARY 4th, 2015

I guess one can say, "What would a conservative talk show be without going for the throat of the Affordable Care Act?" President Obama ran on health-care reform and won not only one but two Presidential elections with the nation fully knowing health-care reform was the primary issue of his candidacy and eventual victories. This has to drive the right-wing absolutely mad. This especially holds true with President Obama winning a second term, which points to one of two things: low voter turnout for the Republicans or the millions of supposed conservatives who listen to Limbaugh don't truly listen to him. The listeners are either not buying the brand of politics he is selling or just don't care about his antics to persuade them enough to drive Democrats out of office and vote Republican. Just look at one of Limbaugh's many rants on the Affordable Care Act or as it is commonly known, Obama Care:

RUSH: *"The House Republicans passed an Obamacare repeal again and the Democrats resort to their same old playbook, which is Republicans hate children, they hate sick people, and they want everybody to die. They're for dirty water and they're for dirty air and they're for poison and all that stuff."* [The Rush Limbaugh Show 2-4-2015]

Can you just see his seething red face and spit flying from the corners of his lips when he discusses things like this? He may be on the radio but I can visualize his disgust and smoldering frown as he expels his reasons as to why the Democrats are bad for the country all the while knowing in the back of his mind that nobody listens to him when he speaks. Think about it. He essentially does the equivalent of a filibuster day in and day out on his show as to why the Democrats have it all wrong yet the last two presidential elections a Democrat has won. I just don't think his ego can take such defeat. Be that as it may, his ego won't let him surrender to the fact that nobody is really, truly accepting his message, nor will he ever admit defeat at the hands of Democrats. He has to come to this conclusion, doesn't he? I've always heard that the definition of insanity is to keep on doing the same thing the same way but expecting a different result. Well, Rush keeps on doing the same thing, spreading hate and discontent towards the Democrats, and getting the same result, a Democrat leading the White House. He has to realize this, but you know what? He will never concede to this idea rather he will make up new and more outlandish excuses as to why Democrats are the evil ones.

Hell, maybe Rush Limbaugh is a closet Democrat. Maybe he does see that what he says doesn't matter and Democrats keep winning which is why he keeps doing things the same way and getting the same results. Democrats in office are maybe what he truly wants. If this is the case, which we all can concede that it isn't, I say keep on doing what you're doing and in the exact same way, Mr. Limbaugh.

"The modern conservative is engaged in one of man's oldest exercises in moral philosophy: that is, the search for a superior moral justification for selfishness."

~John Kenneth Galbraith

DAY 5

FEBRUARY 5th, 2015

Did you know that Rush was great and powerful? No seriously, he says so. If he says it, it must be true. Just look at this comment he made during his broadcast on Day 5 of my conservative radio show undertaking:

RUSH: *"MSNBC has just had its lowest ratings ever, a maximum of 55,000 people. Do you realize there are more people going to the bathroom at one time in this country than are watching MSNBC? And, by the way, this all happens to coincide with my ban on playing any sound bites from that network. I played a role in this, folks."* [The Rush Limbaugh Show 2-5-2015]

He actually takes credit for MSNBC's poor ratings. He, the great and powerful Rush, is the reason for bad ratings now or at least as it pertains to a left-leaning network. The self-admiration this man possesses is astonishing. When I heard this, I actually stopped my car for a moment and asked if he really just took credit for this. I know that at this point nothing should surprise me but the audacity this man displays is redefining. However, after a few seconds of pondering his audacity I realized that his shenanigans are simply a hook for his audience to bite on. He wants them to believe that what he says matters and matters to the point that it affects an entire networks rating. While the ratings he speaks of are in fact accurate, I could not find one article where the ratings drop was due either directly or in part to Limbaugh's refusal to play audio clips from MSNBC. I take that back. I did come across articles where they reported how Rush took credit for the ratings drop but again, not a shred of evidence did I find that points to his show being the true reason. Now could it be that the people in general are fed up with the political atmosphere to the point where they don't want to watch? Could it be that people would rather read and/or watch the network news of the day via computer, tablet, or some other electronic means? I believe that all of these things and more lead to poor ratings from time to time for any network. This buffoon tries to get his listening audience to believe otherwise. Sadly, from what I gathered after my time listening to this show thus far and the audience members who call in, they do believe this to be the case. In my opinion, I think it's safe to say that if you were to look up the definition of arrogance, you would see his picture with the caption that says, "Listen to this guy."

"Snark is the idiots version of wit and we're being polluted by it

~Will McAvoy

DAY 6

FEBRUARY 6th, 2015

Ahh, Day 6 of my expedition into conservative talk radio and I remember thinking to myself, "I can't possibly listen to 24-more days of this rubbish." As the show begins, I feel a slight cringe at the sound of ole Limbaugh's voice, but my morbid curiosity gets me through and I listen on. The segment that intrigues me on this day is Rush going after NBC reporter Brian Williams. If you don't recall, the story is of Brian Williams lying about being on a helicopter that was shot down by enemy fire while reporting in Iraq in 2003. Let me be clear, I am in no way defending Brian Williams and you know damn well Rush isn't, but he turns the story into the ever on-going argument that exists on his show that it's the entire Democrat populous that are the liars and exploiters of everything negative in the news. During yet another tirade, which by the way is the embodiment of his show, he says:

RUSH: *"....As I say, pick your journalist and pick your episode of suffering and ask yourself, "What do they do to solve it?" They don't. They advance a political agenda when they see suffering. They blame their political opponents for it. They blame the Republicans or they blame talk radio or they blame whoever is the villain of the day. They look at the suffering, and they wring their hands, and they chide all of us. "How dare* *you allow this to happen! How dare we permit this to happen!"* [The Rush Limbaugh Show 2-6-2015]

Did you all know that we as liberals thrive on suffering and do nothing about it? Yeah, neither did I. We are not the party out there on daily basis calling for an end to social programs and regulating arms of the government, they are. Rush is just a wordsmith who uses his craft to advance his own political agenda which is simply to disparage every issue that Democrats care about. His statements weren't about Brian Williams, rather they were yet another porthole for Rush to belittle Democrats and liberalism.

Limbaugh's use of the term "chide" struck a chord in me as well. This is where I say the proof is in the proverbial pudding but what Limbaugh does all day and every day is "chide" liberalism. He scolds Democrats at every turn. For example, a person could save a kitten from a burning fire and if Rush discovered that this person was a liberal, he would say that the liberal probably started the fire in the first place and that saving the cat was a diversionary tactic to steer the media away from the real liberal issues that need the attention. This is the entire premise of his show and you cannot convince me otherwise.

And by the way Mr. Limbaugh, when Democrats do make efforts to fix things or improve things for the betterment of our great nation, you "chide" us for making the attempt. What are you doing to make this world a better place? You drone on and on about how we as democrats thrive on suffering while making the claim that we really don't solve anything in the process. My question to Limbaugh would be, "What on God's green Earth are you solving during your three hour daily tenure on the airwaves? What political problems are you solving?" None. The answer is none. He does not offer any resolution other than to bash the democrats while not offering any substantive reason why the conservative way of thinking is better other than simply saying democrats are bad, conservatives are good. While as Archaic and caveman-esque this statement may sound, it is true. This is the sum of his show, near as I can tell.

"We can no longer tolerate anti-intellectualism. We can no longer tolerate liberal-bashing and we can no longer tolerate the politics of the dumb and the mean."

~Janeane Garofolo

DAY 7

FEBRUARY 9th, 2015

Road trip! My conservative talk radio adventure didn't stop on Day 7, even though my wife and I were taking our four children to a water park in Sandusky, Ohio. As a matter of fact, this gave me the opportunity to just about listen to Limbaugh's entire program as our drive was just over two hours in duration. I figured, "What the hell?" and subjected myself with my family present to this lunacy. I should offer that my children immediately put headphones on and listened to their music. My wife did the same, but not before she could say, "How can you listen to this nonsense?" I tell her that I have an idea for a book to which she responds with a chuckle and says, "Yeah right."

And so the freak show begins and I wonder to myself, "What could possibly be the topics today?" and wouldn't you know it? It was about himself and the insinuation of his greatness. I mean, how else would you take it when you hear the show virtually opening to the following:

RUSH: *"Rush Limbaugh, never, never beating a dead horse on this program. We don't get on one or two things and stick with 'em for the rest of time. We don't beat things -- no topics -- in other words you're not gonna get bored here, folks, and despite what you may think, it isn't predictable, and that's why we continue to grow by leaps and bounds."*
[The Rush Limbaugh Show 2-9-2015]

My personal opinion is that this shows his desperation and points to that just maybe his show is starting to go into the tank due to losing sponsors and/or his audience. I mean why would the self-proclaimed "Big Voice on the Right" have to seemingly defend his show's dialogue? I'll tell you why. It's because he is beating "a dead horse", although he claims that he is not. His shows are nothing more than a Democrat bashing and Obama hating script that does nothing to better our country and the political divide. Limbaugh only makes it worse and I can't be convinced otherwise. Talk about beating a dead horse! This is all he has done since President Obama took office. When you have a guy, Rush Limbaugh, state that he hopes the President fails when he won his first term, you get a pretty good idea of what kind of guy this Limbaugh fella is. The narrative of his show, from my own experience in just seven days of listening, is that President Obama and liberals in general are the do nothing, conservative hating, bad policy making, low information, dead from the neck up political party. I feel comfortable in saying that this my friends, the day in and day out liberal bashing by Rush, is in fact beating a dead horse. The horse in this instance is Democrats and liberalism.

By the way, just to sound a bit hip, I did have a "LOL" moment which to those who may not be familiar with this acronym, it means a "laugh out loud" moment. The reason, well after you read the next quote, you'll understand:

RUSH: *"This program and Fox News represent the last best hope of providing a counter to the common narrative of the day that the left used to be able to choose and to determine."* [The Rush Limbaugh Show 2-9-2015]

I'm snickering now as I'm reminded of this comment because I know damn well Fox is a right leaning network which in and of itself is fine by me. What isn't fine, however, is to think that because I watch a left leaning network such as MSNBC, I'm looked upon as getting my information via a liberal network, therefore, the information has to be wrong and the implication I am among the low information crowd. The nerve and pompousness this man called Rush exhibits is astounding. I guess I could be a wordsmith too and reshape his quote by replacing words here and there and say something like, "My book represents hope that can provide a counter to the common Rush narrative of the day that Rush chooses and determines." Seems to work and make sense, right?

"In this world of sin and sorrow there is always something to be thankful for; as for me, I rejoice that I am not a Republican."

~H. L. Mencken

DAY 8

FEBRUARY 10th, 2015

RUSH: *"Do you realize everything that comes out of this administration is dire pessimism, apocalyptic, negative?"* [The Rush Limbaugh Show 2-10-2015]

There you have it folks. Rush sums up the current administration's way of communications in one sentence. I guess the increase in jobs numbers, lower gas prices, the stock market increases, etc. are all negative. I can tell you one thing, this one quote from the Big Mouth on the Right is pretty much the whole of his own show. All you have to do is refer to the previous quotes I offer from day's one through seven to see that the common theme is bashing liberalism. It makes one wonder if Rush knows the meanings of the words he uses to describe our current administration. Pessimism, apocalyptic, negative? This is the entire premise of the three hours that his voice clogs our national airwaves. I refer you to to the fact that he strongly desired that the newly elected President would fail. I refer you to the instances when Democratic candidates were appointed to various positions where he constantly made the claim that they didn't have the brains and/or experience to fulfill the needs of whatever position it may have been. I refer you to the pessimistic, yes I said pessimistic, outlook he has had for the six years that President Obama and his administration have been in office. I refer you to the negative comments he made about Sandra Fluke. I could go on and on but the bottom line is that the very words he uses to describe the Obama Administration are the very words that could be used to describe the manifestation that which is his radio show.

As the show goes on, the negativity doesn't stop. During his seemingly never ending diatribe, he says,

RUSH: *"He gets up every day, and the first thing they want him to read is the Presidential Daily Brief, and all it is is a document of death that happened in the world overnight. Well, what is he doing by creating these lie-based statistics that are gonna lead to attitudes? This is how you create hatred in people."* [The Rush Limbaugh Show 2-10-2015]

Now, the "He" in this quote is referencing President Obama. I think we can all understand or take for granted that Limbaugh wouldn't be Limbaugh if he didn't say that the statistics provided by the President are, as he says, "lie-based". This is to be expected from this guy. The question I have is where the audacity comes from to regurgitate a statement where he makes such an allegation? Who does he know that would tell him that the Presidential Daily Brief is based on lies? After all, Limbaugh hates Democrats, right? One could assume that since the President is surrounded by

Democrats, Rush wouldn't have access to inside sources because if he did, that would mean he would've had to have befriended a Democrat, right? We all know what happens when we assume so let's not do that. My take is that Rush is simply garnering the attention of his listening audience. He wants his audience to believe that the brief is based on lies and sadly, his audience will hang on his every word. This is his particular angle to which has his audience mesmerized and wanting more. I just don't get it because I can't wait to turn the show off.

My curiosity got the best of me after hearing this drivel so I researched what the Press Briefing was on this day, February 10th, 2015. I went to the White House website at www.whitehouse.gov and searched the archives of the Daily Press Briefing for the aforementioned date. This particular date, the topic of discussion was Kayla Mueller. If you don't remember who she was, I will refresh your memory. Ms. Mueller was an American aid worker who became a hostage of ISIS fighters and ultimately was executed by her captors. I remember watching the news stories on CNN when this occurred. The press briefing on this day was filled with questions about this execution and reporters looking for confirmation of the reasons behind the killing. I would agree that this briefing was very sad and troubling. Kayla was, in fact, a hostage of ISIS and was, in fact, executed according to various news outlets and the press briefing. These facts my friends are not lie-based. One may say, "Well, *the Presidential Daily Briefing is different than the Daily Press Briefing.*" In and of themselves that may be true but if you have ever watched the Daily Press briefing with the Press Secretary, the reporters in attendance are always looking for answers from the President and his Administration via the Press Secretary. This would mean that any answers given directly or indirectly from the President had to have been derived only after the President had in fact been given the Presidential Daily Brief. Makes sense to me but remember, Rush says it's all lie-based. Tell that to the family of Kayla Mueller. Needless to say that after this road trip, I needed another trip, which could be described in two words: Beer Run!

"I have been thinking that I would make a proposition to my Republican friends... that if they will stop telling lies about the Democrats, we will stop telling the truth about them."

~Adlai Stevenson

DAY 9

FEBRUARY 11th, 2015

By now, I am happy that I have made it as far as I have subjecting myself to the show that is known as <u>The Rush Limbaugh Show</u>©. I had already had it in my mind just a few days into listening to this show that I would not last the thirty days that I had planned initially. I'm sure that up to this point, you can see why.

This ninth day my listening journey begins and I could have almost predicted what the show was going to be about, in part anyway. It had been in the news about Comedy Central icon Jon Stewart announcing he was going to retire as the luminary of the Daily Show. Now, this happens not too long after NBC's Brian Williams finds himself in a predicament about being less than truthful during one of his Iraq reporting assignments. As you guessed it, the media frenzy began with the rumors of Mr. Stewart replacing Brian Williams and the questions of whether or not his announced departure from his show was coincidental or a move that would lead him to the William's spot. Here's what the Big Mouth had to say, in part:

RUSH: *"Any supposed, so-called news organization that seriously considered hiring an admitted satirist, who made his bones with fake* news, Jon Stewart, any network seriously considering hiring him to moderate *Meet the Press isn't what it claims to be."* [The Rush Limbaugh Show 2-11-2015]

This type of observation by Rush is not only to be expected, but quite the pattern of what he orchestrates everyday, which is hatred towards liberals. What I found fascinating however is what he says just a short time later which was the following:

RUSH: *"What this program was and is -- this is how it started -- combined two elements that were not combined anywhere else in the media: satire and parodic humor, along with a serious discussion of issues, with the host, being me, maintaining credibility no matter what."* [The Rush Limbaugh Show 2-11-2015]

Do you hear, or should I say, did you just read those few short lines? He implies in the previous quote that Jon Stewart is an admitted satirist, which implies that he would not be seriously considered or qualified for the real news. This is just a preposterous notion, at least in Limbaugh's psyche, right? Well, why would he go onto to say almost in the same breath that his namesake show was premised on satire and parodic humor? The Big Mouth being the host of such a show, his own show, would then also be considered a satirist, correct? One could conclude that Limbaugh is not qualified to do what he does every day on the airwaves. One could imply that Limbaugh shouldn't be taken seriously because he just admitted that he is a satirist and those who possess and display their satirical prowess should not be taken seriously. However, the famous and all powerful Rush uses his twisted wordsmith competence by getting his listeners to believe that although satire is a part of what his show is, his discussion of the issues are genuine and that no matter what erupts from his mouth will maintain credibility. You have to love the audacity and confidence this guy has in his personal abilities. The ego this man possesses has to barely fit in the studio from which his show is produced.

Prior to ending Day 9, I just had to add this quote wherein Rush says,

RUSH: *"Say what you want about Jon Stewart, but he did not teach anybody to think about politics in a different way. Jon Stewart cemented liberal thinking about politics."* [The Rush Limbaugh Show 2-11-2015]

I have my own opinion about this in general and as it pertains to me personally, it is a fact: Listening to Rush Limbaugh has not taught me to think about politics in a different way. He has cemented my liberal thinking about politics and has forever spoiled any chance for me to look at conservatism in any type of favorable light. To this end, I say thank you Mr. Limbaugh. Your everyday rants and raves have convinced me that my decision to choose to be a Democrat has been the right one all along. Although I never doubted or questioned my party affiliation, I am now forever emboldened to remain a liberal democrat.

"The school is the last expenditure upon which America should be willing to economize."

~Franklin D. Roosevelt

DAY 10

FEBRUARY 12th, 2015

So Day 10 was interesting as I now find out that the institution of college cannot even escape the large trap that is Rush's mouth. Yes folks, college, the place for higher education. The place where most parents encourage their children to attend and stress the importance of academic excellence while in high school in order to get accepted into a good college. And now we can say it's a place not safe from the perpetual negativity that is Rush Limbaugh.

Let me set this up for you. The particular discussion on his show came about as the debate over Scott Walker, Governor of Wisconsin, was heating up as to whether or not Walker was qualified for the Presidency because he didn't finish college. This was on many news outlets and in print articles from coast to coast. I'm not here to debate this fact, but what I am here to dispute is what it is that Rush had to say about it. This isn't the entire dialogue of course but he says:

RUSH: *"They have been taught how to mess things up in college. They have been instructed in bureaucracy and sustaining bureaucracy and never solving problems and getting credit for solving problems. They never solve anything. They came out of college."* [The Rush Limbaugh Show 2-12-2015]

Did you know that we pay thousands of dollars in tuition to universities only to have our college student population come out only having learned to mess things up? Yeah, this is the Big Mouth's opinion on higher education. I have heard him in previous shows refer to school as "screwl", which in my own assumption is his made up word that implies that schools are just there to "screw" you. I could be wrong, but this is my opinion as to what he means and my opinion only. I guess I could have researched when he actually said this word and/or what his meaning behind it was but I figured it wasn't worth my energy. OK, so I lied. I did a little research and I found this quote from www.ontheissues.org wherein they quote Limbaugh as saying, *"Limbaugh regularly discourages his listeners from getting an education. He always says "screwls" instead of "schools" to imply that educators are screwing up children."* (Source: <u>The Most Dangerous Man in America, by J.K.Wilson, p. 2-3</u>, Mar 1, 2011)

Please don't misunderstand me here my friends. I am not, nor would I ever call Rush stupid simply because he is not a college graduate. I know this because I have heard him say that he only went to college for a year or something like that. I also would not say that he is not qualified to do his show for this reason. What really gets my blood pressure rising is his statement that all colleges accomplish is producing graduates who know how to mess things up. I am a college graduate, who by the way took advantage of Federal Student Loans, and I take offense to this notion as I'm sure countless others do, as well, to include his listeners.

Want to know an ironic thing that I have heard on his show? There is a higher education institution called Hillsdale College that not only advertises on the Limbaugh show, but Rush is a spokesman for them wherein he encourages his listeners to check them out and look into their classes. Here is my take on all of this. Hillsdale is just using Rush to get to the masses due to his listening base hence the reason behind marketing in general. I find it hard to comprehend that even though Limbaugh makes such a broad comment about "screwls", it would be understood that he means all schools, which would include Hillsdale. How could a higher education establishment use such a figurehead knowing he makes comments like this about such institutions, higher education or otherwise? It escapes my comprehension other than it's simply about attracting enrollment no matter what the cost. This includes the cost of having a radio show host who's known to make outlandish and often controversial comments to be the face of, or in this case, the voice of your college. I guess it boils down to the numbers and by numbers, I mean the almighty dollar.

"It is essential that there should be organization of labor. This is an era of organization. Capital organizes and therefore labor must organize."

~Theodore Roosevelt

DAY 11

FEBRUARY 13th, 2015

What a perfect day to almost end my conservative radio listening quest, Friday the 13th. It's kind of ironic as this date usually sparks fear and uneasiness in people whereas this particular day is when my horror of listening to Limbaugh is nearly coming to an end. Horror may be a strong word, but I have to tell ya, the last few days were hard to get through and this holds true for this day as well.

Unions. The big, scary word that conservatives hate to hear uttered. I know that conservatives are not union supporters and with more and more GOP potential candidates in the news, it's even more prevalent, what, with Scott Walker and all. Although rather docile for the Big Mouth, he said:

RUSH: *"If you work for a union, you're giving up -- I mean, this is just the way it is. If you work for a union you're giving up your individuality. What you get paid is negotiated for you, and you're lumped into a group and you get paid whatever everybody else gets paid, whatever union you're in."* [Source: The Rush Limbaugh Show 2-13-2015]

He is absolutely right when he speaks of union negotiations as it pertains to wages. What he fails to mention is that this is not the only issue negotiated. I'm not only a union member, but I am also a contract negotiator for the union I belong to. During negotiations, we discuss everything from days off, health insurance, wages, seniority, sick time, etc. The list goes on and on as I'm sure you all know. My point is not to bore you with this stuff rather my point is that unions have fought hard to provide a much better living wage and working conditions for its members than maybe a non-union member may experience. It provides job security by equipping the members with protection from unfair labor practices and unsafe working conditions to name a few. Good ole Rush implies that your just a robot of sorts and not an individual. If this were true, why is it individuals seek gainful employment wherein they are offered membership into a union? It's not because they think they'll lose their individuality. It's because they know that they will gain a livable wage, have health benefits, and be protected from unfair and/or unnecessary abuses within the workplace.

Staying within the theme of individualism or seemingly so, later in the program while speaking to a caller, the topic was Republican candidacy and how the GOP should address minority's.

In this instance, they reference the African-American and Hispanic communities. The caller believed that said candidates should address groups instead of individuals. During the back and forth with the caller, the Big Mouth had this to say:

RUSH: *"Whatever Republican consultant (or any consultant, period) tells me is, 'We don't live as individuals anymore. You can't talk to people. You've got to talk to 'em as a member of a group they're in or that they think they're in. And if you don't know how to do that, then you don't have a prayer. A couple of Republican candidates now seeking the presidency have told me that. They've come down here wanting to kiss the ring, and in the conversations, that's what they've all said to me."*
[Source: The Rush Limbaugh Show 2-13-2015]

I've only put this quote in for one reason and it isn't to debate or dispute what he says rather it's to show his arrogance and narcissism. Do you see the last line of this quote? He says "They've come down here wanting to kiss the ring." Wanting to kiss the ring? I know, you're probably thinking to yourself that this has to be a joke but it's not. Apparently, Rush thinks of himself as the Don Corleone of conservatism or should I say the "capo" of the right-wing. Or could it be he thinks himself to be the Pope of the conservative wing? After all, he pontificates on a daily basis about things that only add to the already buzzing media machine rather than solve actual political party agenda issues.

What's disheartening is that the GOP folks not only continue to not call Limbaugh out on his daily antics, they support him as the face of their party. Maybe I'm crazy. You be the judge.

"The legitimate object of government, is to do for a community of people, whatever they need to have done..."

~Abraham Lincoln

DAY 12

FEBRUARY 18th, 2015

My last day. I tried my best folks to listen to an entire 30-days, but I am just too damn tired to listen to this far right leaning drivel anymore. I gave it the ole college try as they say, Rush doesn't say this because he thinks college is for suckers, but most get what I'm driving at. On this day, I hear him refer to a summit that is to be held at The White House as some sort of ISIS jobs summit. I'll explain in a moment but this is part of hat he had to say:

RUSH: *"First thing to do is a White House jobs summit. They're doing this three day shindig and they're calling it Countering Violent Extremism summit. Why not just turn it into another jobs summit? I mean, Marie Harf and Obama think getting ISIS people jobs is the best way to counter extremism. Maybe, in addition to doing that, you could bring in the Chamber of Commerce. Maybe bring in the Chamber of Commerce as a weapon of mass destruction against ISIS."* [Source: The Rush Limbaugh Show 2-18-2015]

Before I get into the sheer ignorance that are his comments, I'll detail the reasons behind his nonsensical comments.

This particular week when Rush made these comments, The White House hosted a three day summit aptly referred to as the Countering Violent Extremism summit. It was a way to get all those folks charged with keeping our country and the global community protected together and work towards a plan to counteract the violent extremists, both foreign and domestic. The people in attendance were local, state and foreign leaders to include President Obama. Great idea, in my humble opinion, but I'll explain a little more.

The reason for ole Limbaugh's sarcasm is not necessarily the summit itself but comments made my State Department spokeswoman, Marie Harf. She was apparently on MSNBC's Hardball with Chris Mathews© and made comments about how we should focus on getting ISIS members employment or something to this effect. In keeping with my theme, you guessed it, I researched and found what Ms. Harf said or at least what Rush says her statement was. She, according to Rush, made the statement; "*We cannot win the War on Terror, nor can we win the war on ISIS by killing them. We need to find them jobs. We need to get to the root cause of terrorism, and that is poverty and lack of opportunity in the terrorist community."* [Source: The Rush Limbaugh Show 2-17-2015]

Now you all know what led to Rush's ignorance as he turned a positive reason for a summit in Washington D.C into a conservative's attempt at being a comedian. This is what he does folks. He turns positive, liberal-led ideas and gatherings into a negative, political comedy show. In his eyes, he believes he is funny and making a great point where in reality, he is putting a negative spin on something that is really needed in our great country and across the globe, which is unity in fighting terrorism. I am not saying that I agree with Ms. Harf's comments and in full disclosure, I did not see any of the show in which she made the comments. I'm near positive there is more to it, but in true Rush fashion, he only tells a small piece of the actual entire story and spins it to represent the whole of what was said. I guess he is guilty of the same acts of reporting as he accuses what he calls "the drive-by's" when referring to national media. I guess you could say that Rush is the epitome of the very practices he says are wrong by which the national media operates. This could make him the "drive-by" talk radio host of our national airwaves.

Ted Cruz Announces Run For Presidency

MARCH 23rd, 2015

These next few chapters I decided to add as I anticipated interesting dialogue to flow from Rush as candidates announced their bid for President of the United States. I couldn't resist listening to the Big Mouth on this date. Not because I find Rush so appealing that I couldn't resist his arrogant, egotistical, and sometimes vulgar persona. That's not it at all. I was simply curious as to what he had to say about Senator Ted Cruz having officially declared his candidacy for President. I most certainly couldn't resist when Hillary Clinton announced, which you will see in the chapter that follows this one. And, oh my goodness, let the madness begin.

Topics abound during this show, but of course one main topic was Cruz compared to President Obama as it pertains to qualifications to be President. During one of his ramblings he says,

RUSH: *"I'm talking about Ted Cruz. Did you ever stop and look at Ted Cruz that way? Some guy that's only been a senator for a short time, some guy with not any real executive experience, biggest qualification, went to Harvard Law School, foreign name, mixed ethnic background, questions about his birth certificate. Yeah, I saw it on CNN today. He may not be qualified. He might have been born in Canada. It is uncanny.*

Everything about Barack Obama that they said qualified him they are saying disqualifies Ted Cruz." [Source: The Rush Limbaugh Show 3-23-2015]

I can say that I do remember when President Obama was running, the debate was his lack of experience and who could forget the whole "birther" issue. If you don't recall, "birther" was a term born out of those folks out there who say President Obama wasn't born here in the United States.

Rush, in my opinion, and though he doesn't come out and say it, appears to be a fan of Mr. Cruz for President. I've heard him in the past say he will never actually come out on air and support any one candidate. So to the Big Mouth I say this, "Why is it that all I've heard you say in the shows that I've listened to is how bad of a job President Obama is doing and yet you imply that Mr. Cruz is qualified to run our great nation, even though his qualifications are similar to President Obama's?" The answer is not only simple but predictable as it would be this, "he is a conservative". Rush and his minions hate liberals so much that they would take the far right Cruz fellow no matter the cost to our country, specifically the middle class. Not that I'm a fan of Jeb Bush but he, in Rush's eye, is not conservative enough. That's what's so comical to me. Rush and his followers even abhor those who consider themselves conservatives because they're not conservative enough. In other words, if they don't exhibit and/or share the exact same opinions and conservative values that Limbaugh lives and breathes, they aren't good conservatives. I've heard conservatives refer to such people as a "RINO" or Republican In Name Only and also as the "inside the beltway Republicans", which in the context he uses these terms is meant to bare a negative connotation is his little world.

As the show carries on and I continue to willingly subject my delicate auditory senses to this ignorance and narcissism, he goes on to say,

RUSH: *"You contrast what exists on the Republican side with the vanilla that's on the Democrat side, I don't care who you pick, Hillary, Elizabeth Warren, Joe Biden, take your pick of any of them over there, and all you've got is Chairman Mao Jr. I mean, you don't have any diversity on the left whatsoever. You've got far left, extreme left, and nothing else."*
[Source: The Rush Limbaugh Show 3-23-2015]

Vanilla? Did he just use a word that liberal hipsters use quite frequently? Yes, I believe he did. In any event, does he really believe that the conservatives out there really offer something so exciting and world changing that a makes them in a league of their own? He can't really believe this. I could very easily change a few words and it would read "You've got GOP establishment, far right, extreme right and nothing else." This holds true and he knows it but he will never admit this. The whole premise of his show's existence is to bash liberalism and those who align themselves with liberal beliefs. If he were to ever dare take a shot at what he calls "true conservatives" and call them out on some of their antics, it would probably mean the beginning of the end of his show. He knows this, which is why I said before I would never say or accuse him of being dumb. I completely reject his take on everything political. Hell, I reject just about everything that comes out of his mouth, but would never say he is a stupid person.

Finally, and far more laughable, is his comparison of potential Democratic candidates to Chair Mao Jr. To refresh your memories, Chair Mao was the Chinese Communist leader and founding father of the People's Republic of China. I say the Big Mouth's comment is laughable, but I really should use the term predictable. I could predict that no matter who the Democratic candidate may be, they will be referred to by Rush as a Socialist, Communist and/or Marxist as this is his method of operation or M.O. I've heard him say this before about President Obama and adds that the President is a socialist. You know, I've heard Limbaugh say that all liberals do is spread fear and hate yet he refers to members of the Democratic party as being communists. If this isn't the definition of trying to scare people into switching their political views and affiliations, I don't know what is. Most people who I know of consider Communism, Marxism, etc., something that should not be tolerated nor should it be as it pertains to those who lead us. How could Rush accuse liberals of aligning themselves with these principles and values while keeping a straight face? I'll tell you why. Ratings. It's all about entertaining his audience to get them to come back each and every day wanting more of his_outlandish comments and monologues. I would even go as far as to say that he is simply an entertainer who is good at delivering a dialogue that keeps his audience wondering what he is going to say next. That's all it is. A perverted, conservative form of entertainment, plain and simple.

HILLARY CLINTON ANNOUNCES PRESIDENTIAL CANDIDACY

APRIL 13th, 2015

The real, final day of my painful journey of listening to the King of all narcissists, Rush Limbaugh. I knew that what he would have to say about Hillary Clinton announcing her candidacy for President would be epic in the sense that he would let his anger, frustration and fear shine right through. Yes, I said fear because he, like all conservatives, knows that their GOP field of candidates is weak and that Mrs. Clinton will probably win by a landslide, no matter the opponent. And of course, as I predicted, his anger and fear was ever evident. You could almost see the veins in his head through the airwaves pulsing like a python that just swallowed a rat. Here was his reaction as he stated:

RUSH: *"I Don't Care About Hillary's Campaign.... I angrily, actively don't care about Mrs. Clinton and her presidential announcement and her campaign and everything associated. I don't care what the media is saying about it. I don't care who's excited. I don't care a whit about it."* [Source: The Rush Limbaugh Show 4-12-2015]

Does this reaction actually surprise any of you? It sure didn't surprise me one iota. If there is one thing I swiftly learned while listening to this dolt is that he is just an angry conservative who thrives on finding fault in every little thing a liberal accomplishes. Of course he doesn't care about a liberal announcing for President. He makes it sound like he doesn't care about Hillary when the fact of the matter is that he doesn't care about any liberal out there. To him we are all uninformed, naive supporters who align themselves with the democratic party. Yeah, he doesn't care about Hillary or her campaign nor does he care about any upright, breathing liberal out there. Or does he? I'll explain this in a few moments but as Limbaugh continues on his tirade, he goes on to say:

RUSH: *"Mrs. Clinton hasn't the slightest idea, and neither does Barack Obama and most in the Democrat Party, despite their claim they stand for the little guy, they really don't know what everyday Americans, ordinary Americans...they have no idea what life his like for most people today."* [Source: The Rush Limbaugh Show 4-13-2015]

I found myself saying out loud while listening to this, "You have got to be kidding me." Does this guy really, truly expect his listeners to believe that he knows what ordinary Americans experience on a daily basis? Does he really believe that he knows what life is like for everyday working people in our great country? I say "hell no he doesn't!" He sits behind that phallic symbol of a microphone and spews his complete and utter animosity for liberals all the while collecting his millions a year from his sponsors. Golfing every day and smoking cigars after sitting in front of a microphone for three hours is not how the everyday, average American spends their days. Don't tell me you know what ordinary people have to deal with on a daily basis, Mr. Limbaugh, while you're jet setting to different destinations to play golf or make celebrity appearances with your conservative bedfellows. You play your part to engage your audience all the while knowing you're simply an entertainer aimed to please your conservative audience. It's nothing more than you being a conservative figure head and a ploy to keep you relevant in the media. To use a phrase I've heard you use, "I'm not drinking the kool-aid you're selling Mr. Limbaugh."

I'll now go back and answer the question from a few paragraphs ago when I ended by implying that maybe Rush does care about liberals. The answer is that he must care about Hillary and I'll tell you why. After finishing this final day of listening to this show, I came up with the idea to listen to Limbaugh's radio show when I had the time during the week of April 20th, 2015. I did this because it was a week after Hillary announced and I wanted to see just how much Rush didn't care about her announcing, what the media had to say, and all the other things he said he didn't care about on the day after she announced. I actually kept a log of sorts just keeping track of how much he didn't care about Hillary's campaign. From April 20th, 2015 through April 23rd, 2015 I am able to report to you that Rush really does care about Hillary and her campaign. Just in the short time that I caught his show during the four days I reference, I came up with a tally of 48-minutes of air time that he used not caring about Hillary. When I say he cares, he really cares.

In those 48-minutes spread across four days, he spoke of Hillary's campaign, what the media was reporting, her appearance, her age, her ankles or as he referred to them as her "cankles", The Clinton Foundation, Bill Clinton himself, Whitewater and the list goes on. He not only cares about Hillary, he was up to his waist in material just discussing her campaign. As I quoted before, Limbaugh says he doesn't care a "whit" about Hillary and her campaign. Well, I can tell you that based upon what I heard this particular week, he not only cares but he might be in love with her.

A SHORT LIST OF NOT-SO-FUNNY "RUSH"
TERMINOLOGY

As promised and before wrapping up the book, I compiled a list of some of the phrases and let's say "creative" words that I heard Limbaugh use during his shows. The following list is nowhere near all-inclusive and the definitions that follow said words is the definition I assigned based upon the context in which I heard them used. They are my own definitions that I crafted and not an official definition. Get ready to observe conservative ignorance at a whole new level.

Drive-By Media- I heard this too many times to count flow from his mouth like an erupting volcano. This term is what is used to describe pretty much any media source that may defend and/or align themselves with Democrats and liberalism in general.

Feminazi- used against to describe feminists in our country however with the implication that their beliefs and tactics are of Nazi influence. One of many ways the Big Mouth on the Right shows his love for liberal women.

Half my brain tied behind my back- A <u>Rush Limbaugh Show</u>© slogan of sorts saying he is only using half of his brain and yet smarter than his audience.

Screwl- When I first heard this, I wasn't sure what he was implying. As the days went on, I heard this used a few more times which it became apparent that it meant people who are going to school are only getting screwed. Of course, the almighty Rush thinks education in this country is in the toilet because of liberalism so why not preach it from his air wave pulpit.

The list I describe could probably be so long as to warrant its own book but these particular ones really touched a nerve. Hell, just about everything he had to say strummed away at every last nerve in my body. I just can't wrap my head around the appeal this man has and why he has the audience size that he does. I just can't figure it out.

WRAPPING

IT UP

So why did I write this book? People have told me that I shouldn't even give the time of day to listening to <u>The Rush Limbaugh Show</u>© as it only adds to his audience numbers and increased ratings. While I can agree with that sentiment, I felt compelled to have my voice be heard about the ignorance that is his shows political argument. To put it simply, I wrote this book because I became inspired to speak out against what Rush stands for. I don't expect to win any literary awards for this work rather it was my way to allow others to relate to the opinions I have shared. The political climate in this day and age is frustrating to bare witness to say the least. Truthfully, I could have listened to any conservative talk show host and I have in the past but Limbaugh strikes a chord with my liberal-leaning thinking. I've listened to the likes of Bill Cunningham, Hugh Hewitt, the Fox News© cast of characters, etc. and they have never stirred up political emotion the way that Rush Limbaugh does. Yes, not even <u>Fox News</u>©, although they are a close second. I'm not one of these people out here trying to get Rush to stop what he's doing or things like that. I'm just trying to convey the message that what he has to say is nothing more than negative, ignorant rants about the Democrat party. He does not offer solutions to the very things he thinks Liberals are doing poorly. He just says our country is heading in a downward spiral and it's because he hates the fact that the Obama Administration is Democratic. He pontificates on this daily because it's what his audience craves. I've heard conservatives talk about getting rid of the Department of Education, the EPA, the IRS, and the list goes on. As a matter of fact, I heard on a local show where a caller's idea was to get rid of the Federal Reserve and then the government in its entirety. Now, I'm sure he was just trying to garner a chuckle but the callers who dial in to the daily Limbaugh fiasco are ones who would say things such as the caller I mention only they would mean it wholeheartedly. I just don't understand how he has the following he does. The callers align themselves with the abhoration Rush has for Democrats that he displays on a daily basis. The whole premise of his show is to demonize the Democrat party. He makes up childish nicknames for everybody he disagrees with, Democrats. He uses one word to describe every Democratic nominee for any office in the Obama Administration, unqualified. He has droned on and on that the Democrats made up the war on women yet refers to Ms. Fluke as slut for trying to incorporate birth control into college health plans. These are just a few examples, but one thing remains the same. In my brief experience listening, Rush never offers solutions nor does he offer up a conservative leader who could take control and make our great nation a better place. The very nation he claims to love yet exudes his desire for a newly elected President to fail.

The idea behind this so-called great voice on the right is an elementary one. He doesn't openly support any one candidate, which is actually a smart idea and here's why. If the candidate he would support or endorse should screw up, lose the election, make a fool of themselves during debates, etc., Rush would then have to defend his decision to support said candidate. He doesn't want to do that because it would badly bruise that ever growing ego of his because he claims to be too smart for things like that . You can get an idea of who he would support but he, in my short tenure as a listener, would never come out and say he is supporting any single candidate. He simply supports whoever is not the liberal Democrat. That's his M.O. Hating democrats and his self-proclaiming knowledge of knowing Democrats better than they know themselves is what his entire radio operation is about. Nothing more and nothing less.

By the way, I happened to catch a segment of his show while finishing this very last chapter. Are you ready for this? Because it relates to what I quoted him as saying back on Day 7. If you recall, he gloats about how he and his show doesn't ever "beat a dead horse" on his program. On April 28th, 2015 the Big Mouth erupts with the following and I quote,

RUSH: *"That's after we have made a black overweight woman the richest TV entertainer in the country: Oprah. And how's that work out for you? We have the first African-American president, and they, the African-Americans, are as unhappy, ticked off, and angry as ever.* **I don't mean to keep beating a dead horse with this**, *but it's important to realize this. It didn't work."* (Source: The Rush Limbaugh Show 4-28-2015)

As I'm sure you notice, the line that jumps out at you is the one that proves that he really doesn't mean what he says on his program. He just follows the narrative of his show to continue to garner new sponsors, make his millions, have his callers feed his ever hungry ego all the while it is obvious that he is an entertainer and is so at the expense of the Democratic party.

By the way, as I type this last page on October 14th, 2015 I can report that Rush is still talking about Hillary Clinton and her campaign on his show. So much for not caring about her and her Presidential campaign, right?

Thanks for allowing me to share my thoughts and opinions with you as I offered my take on conservative talk radio. I am very happy, or should I say ecstatic to report, that I am still a Democrat, Conservative Talk Radio Didn't Change That!

REFERENCES

-The Rush Limbaugh Show© 2015-live radio shows

-www.rushlimbaugh.com/daily -Archive of the shows manuscripts.

-http://www.addictinginfo.org/2013/06/16/50-quotes-americans-should-remember/-accessed 11-5-2015

-http://www.wisdomquotes.com/topics/liberals/index2.html-accessed 11-5-2015